Bouquet de
BRETAGNE

Bouquet de

BRETAGNE

Seasonal Recipes from
Le Bretagne, Questembert

GEORGES PAINEAU

PAVILION

First published in Great Britain in 1993 by
PAVILION BOOKS LIMITED
196 Shaftesbury Avenue, London WC2H 8JL

Designed by Janet James

ISBN 1 85145 7887

Printed and bound in Singapore
by Tien Wah Press

2   4   6   8   10   9   7   5   3   1

This book may be ordered by post
direct from the publisher. Please
contact the Marketing Department.
But try your bookshop first.

CONTENTS

Spring in Brittany is the season of light. It is the patches of light and dark shadows in the burgeoning forest, contrasts also found in the marketplace, where the freshness and perfume of the first spring vegetables from around Léon and the Val Nantais have begun to replace winter's tired offerings.

This is the time when the lively fish markets re-open, from Trégor to Cornouaille and from the windswept Pointe du Raz in Finistère to the gentle Golfe du Morbihan along the south coast.

Once again broom and gorse bloom wildly. Pursuits that were set aside for winter are taken up again. Cooking is infused with new life, too, with the rising of the sap.

It is the season of calm seas. Small boats set off to gather from the sandy bottom their harvest of seafood, now bursting with roe. Salt-marsh lambs are led out to join black and white cattle in pastures where the sturdier animals have been grazing all winter long.

Spring brings the rebirth of cooking, left to lie fallow during winter. It prompts the rediscovery of ingredients from both the land and the sea in the rich cuisine of Brittany.

MENUS

Oysters in Seaweed Cream
Crème d'algues aux huîtres de pleine mer

Scallop Raviolis with Herbs
Les ravioles de pétoncles aux herbes

Roast Rack of Lamb
Carré d'agneau de 'pré salé' rôti

Spring Vegetables
Jeunes légumes de printemps

Terrine of Oranges with Kiwi Fruit Sauce
La terrine d'oranges au coulis de kiwis

———————

Pasta with Lobster and Chicken Livers
Macaronade de langouste aux foies de volaille

Sole with Tomato Sauce
La sole au plat au coulis de tomates

Roast Pigeon with Garlic
Pigeonneaux farcis à l'ail

Vegetable Compote
Légumes en compote

Chocolate Fondant Cake
Fondant au chocolat

OYSTERS IN SEAWEED CREAM

Crème d'algues aux huîtres de pleine mer

SERVES 4

20 oysters
100g/3½oz edible seaweed preserved in brine, or 7g/¼oz dried
seaweed
600ml/1 pint/2⅓ cups crème fraîche or whipping cream
1½ tbsp cold butter, cut in pieces
freshly ground pepper

U sing an oyster knife (a short wide blade with a protective hilt), open the oysters over a bowl to recuperate the liquid inside. Hold the oyster in a cloth with the flat side up, push the knife into the hinge and around the edge to sever the muscle, which will allow the top shell to be pried off. When all the oysters have been opened, strain the liquid through a sieve lined with muslin which has been rinsed and wrung dry. Remove the oysters from their shells, rinse in cold running water, removing any adhering bits of shell, and return them to the filtered oyster liquid.

If using preserved seaweed, drain well. If using dried seaweed, soak in cold water for at least 10 minutes to rehydrate, rinse and drain. Cut the seaweed across the leaves into very thin ribbons. If the seaweed is not tender, simmer for about 5–10 minutes, depending on thickness, until tender, then drain.

In a heavy saucepan, combine the cream with 5 tbsp of the filtered oyster liquid. Bring to a boil, reduce the heat and add the seaweed. Cook gently for about 8 minutes, or until the cream is reduced and thickened. Add the oysters to the cream with the butter. Swirl the saucepan to incorporate the butter. Remove the oysters with a slotted spoon as soon as they are heated through, about 1 minute, and divide them among 4 warmed soup plates. Cover with the seaweed cream, apportioning the seaweed evenly. Season with freshly ground pepper.

Note: If seaweed is not obtainable, spinach leaves cut in thin ribbons make an attractive alternative, although not a substitute. Spinach needs no precooking.

SCALLOP RAVIOLIS WITH HERBS

Les ravioles de pétoncles aux herbes

SERVES 4

200g/7oz/1½ cups plain (all-purpose) flour
½ tsp salt, plus more for seasoning
2 medium eggs
2 egg whites
48 bay scallops or 24 queen scallops, without coral
pepper
500ml/16fl oz/2 cups reduced fish stock (see page 20) [Sole with Tomato Sauce]
1½ tbsp butter
2 tbsp chopped fresh tarragon
2 tbsp chopped fresh chives

Make the pasta dough in advance. Put the flour, salt, eggs and egg whites in a food processor and mix until they form a ball. Remove, dust with flour, wrap tightly in a tea towel or plastic bag and refrigerate several hours or overnight. To make the raviolis, cut the pasta dough in quarters. Working with one quarter at a time so it does not dry out, roll the dough as thinly as possible, either using a pasta machine or by hand. Cut 24 rounds with a 6cm/2½ inch round pastry cutter. Any remaining dough may be used for another purpose.

Sprinkle the scallops with salt and pepper. Put 2 bay scallops or 1 queen scallop on each round just off centre. Moisten the edge lightly with water and fold in half to enclose the scallops, forming a crescent shape. Press the edges to seal and flatten the double layer of pasta at the edge. Allow them to dry a few minutes, not touching one another. Bring a large pot of salted water to a boil, add the raviolis and boil for 6 minutes or until the pasta is just tender. Drain the raviolis as soon as they are cooked.

Meanwhile, heat the reduced fish stock to the boiling point. Swirl in the pieces of butter one at a time, adjust the seasoning and add the chopped herbs. Divide the cooked raviolis between 4 warmed soup plates, ladle the sauce over them and serve immediately.

Notes: If large eggs are used, only 1 egg white will be necessary for the pasta dough.

The scallops may be enclosed in the raviolis several hours ahead. Refrigerate the formed pasta in one layer or in several layers with greaseproof paper between.

ROAST RACK OF LAMB

Carré d'agneau de 'pré salé' rôti

SERVES 4

2 racks of lamb, total weight about 1.25-1.5kg/2½–3lb, trimmed
¾ tsp salt
¾ tsp pepper
½ tsp curry powder
olive oil, for brushing
2 tbsp red wine or port (optional)
200ml/7fl oz lamb stock or water

T he racks should be French trimmed to leave the ends of the bones bare. Ask the butcher for the trimmings and any bones. Score the outer layer of fat lightly. Mix together the salt, pepper and curry powder. Brush the lamb with a little olive oil and sprinkle with the spice mixture. Let stand up to 1 hour until ready to cook.

Preheat the oven to 220°C/425°F/gas mark 7. Place the meat, fat side up, with any trimmings in a roasting pan and roast for 25–30 minutes for medium-rare (about 50°C/125°F on a meat thermometer), or a few minutes longer for more well-done meat.

When the lamb is cooked, remove and keep warm. Add the wine, if wished, and stock or water to the drippings in the roasting pan. Boil gently for 4–5 minutes, scraping up the brown bits from the bottom of the pan. Strain the sauce and remove the fat.

Arrange the two racks on a warmed serving platter with the ends of the bones interlocking to form an arch. Decorate the bones with paper frills, if wished. Serve the sauce separately.

Notes: Using stock rather than water will give the sauce more flavour. To make a simple lamb stock, brown the trimmings and bones with a coarsely chopped onion and carrot over a moderately high heat. Add 2 crushed garlic cloves, a bouquet garni, and 300ml/10fl oz/1¼ cups water. Bring to a boil, turn down the heat and simmer about ½ hour. If there are no bones and few trimmings, add a lamb or beef stock cube with the water.

SPRING VEGETABLES

Jeunes légumes de printemps

SERVES 4

225g/½ lb carrots
225g/½ lb turnips
225g/½ lb small new potatoes
4-5 tbsp butter
salt and pepper
750g/1½ lb young peas, shelled (about 200g/7 oz/1¼ cups
shelled peas)

Peel the carrots and turnips, halve or quarter them lengthways and cut them into sticks. Peel the potatoes, if wished. Sauté the potatoes in 2–3 tbsp of the butter over a moderate heat for 25 minutes, or until tender. Season with salt and pepper.

Meanwhile, cook the carrots and turnips in 2 tbsp each of water and butter, covered, for 15 minutes, or until tender. Cook the peas in boiling salted water for 15 minutes. Season all the vegetables with salt and pepper to taste.

To serve, arrange the cooked vegetables on the platter with the meat or combine them in a warmed serving bowl.

Note: If frozen peas are used, add them to the carrots and turnips for about the last 4 minutes of cooking.

TERRINE OF ORANGES
WITH KIWI FRUIT SAUCE

La terrine d'oranges au coulis de kiwis

SERVES 4

8 large naval oranges
2 tbsp powdered gelatine (unflavored gelatin) or 8 sheets of
gelatine
500ml/16fl oz/2 cups orange juice (from about 6 oranges)
6 ripe kiwi fruits, peeled and quartered
100g/3¹/₂oz/7 tbsp sugar
fruit, for serving (strawberries, raspberries, blueberries,
redcurrants, etc)
mint leaves, for serving

P eel the oranges, removing all the white pith.
Holding them over a bowl to recuperate the juice,
cut the fruit from between the membranes, and
compress the remains to extract the juice. Drain off the
juice from the orange sections into a small saucepan or
the top of a double-boiler. If using powdered gelatine,
sprinkle the gelatine evenly over the surface of the juice.
Let stand for about 2 minutes or until the granules

become translucent, then place the saucepan in a larger shallow pan of simmering water or assemble the double-boiler. Heat gently until the gelatine is completely dissolved, stirring occasionally. If using gelatine sheets, soak them in cold water until soft, squeeze out excess water and heat in the juice to dissolve.

Stir the hot orange juice with the dissolved gelatine into the cold juice. Pour a thin layer, about 1cm/⅜ inch, into the bottom of a long narrow terrine made of metal or enamelled cast-iron with a capacity of 1.25 litres/2 pints/5 cups. Refrigerate until it is set, about 15 minutes, and keep the remaining juice in the refrigerator as well.

When the first layer of orange jelly (gelatin) is set, arrange a layer of oranges close together on top and spoon on a little more juice to just cover the fruit. Refrigerate until set, cover with another layer of fruit, a little more of the partially set juice and continue until all the ingredients are used. If the orange jelly (gelatin) starts to set too quickly before it can be layered with the fruit, remove it from the refrigerator, stir briskly and keep in a warm place; it is difficult to layer if it becomes thicker than softly whipped cream. Cover the filled terrine and refrigerate at least 4 hours or overnight.

To make the kiwi sauce, purée the kiwi fruits with the sugar in a food processor or food mill. Refrigerate until serving.

To serve, cut the terrine into fairly thick slices and arrange on chilled dessert plates. Surround with the kiwi fruit sauce and garnish with fruit and mint leaves.

The spring in Bretagne is more genial than in the environs of Paris, and the blossoms are more than three weeks in advance . . . The ground was clad with daisies, pansies, jonquils, narcissus, hyacynths, ranunculus, anemones. The glades were diversified with the blended tints of tall and elegant firs, intermingled with the flowers of the broom and the furze, so brilliant that they might have been mistaken for gold-winged butterflies. The hedges, which abounded with wild strawberries, raspberries and sweet smelling violets, were decked with the hawthorn, honeysuckle and briar, whose dark and entwining stems were covered with blossoms and magnificent foliage. Bees, birds and butterflies animated every place; and the numerous birds' nests arrested the steps of children at every turn. Here and there, in some sheltered spot, the laurel-rose and the myrtle flourished in the open air as in Greece; the fig-tree yielded its fruit as in Provence, and every apple-tree, with its carmine flowers, resembled the bouquet of a village bride.

CHATEAUBRIAND *Mémoires d'Outre-Tombe*

PASTA WITH LOBSTER AND CHICKEN LIVERS

Macaronade de langouste aux foies de volaille

SERVES 4

1.2kg/2½lb live lobster
6 whole chicken livers (12 pieces)
salt and pepper
280g/9oz fresh pasta or 250g/8oz dried pasta shapes
7 tbsp butter
150ml/5fl oz/⅔ cup crème fraîche or whipping cream
1 tbsp Dijon mustard

Put the lobster in a large quantity of rapidly boiling salted water and cook for 15 minutes. When cool enough to handle, remove the tail and extract the meat. After breaking off the claws and legs, crack the claws and remove the meat, as well as that from the body.

Trim any fat or nerves from the chicken livers and cut out any greenish areas. Separate them if attached in pairs. Season with salt and pepper.

Cook the pasta in a large amount of boiling salted water until just tender, about 3-4 minutes for fresh pasta or longer for dried pasta (see package instructions). Drain and rinse the pasta.

Meanwhile sauté the chicken livers in 2 tbsp of the

butter over a moderately high heat for about 2 minutes on each side. They should still be pink. Remove and drain on paper towels.

Heat the cream, mustard and the remaining butter in a large saucepan over a moderate heat for 5 minutes, whisking to combine well. Add the pasta and cook long enough to heat through, then transfer to a warmed ovenproof serving platter or baking dish. Cut the lobster tail meat into 16 slices. Arrange the chicken livers and lobster meat on the pasta and put in a preheated 120°C/250°F/gas mark ½ oven for 2–3 minutes to reheat all the components, then serve immediately.

Alternatively, add the lobster meat and the chicken livers to the pasta and sauce, heat through and divide among 4 warmed serving plates.

Notes: This recipe may be halved for 2 servings. Use 1 lobster weighing 750g/1½lb or 1 lobster tail. Smaller lobsters require about 10–12 minutes cooking time.

The lobster may be cooked ahead and refrigerated, but it will need more time for reheating, best effected by adding it to the pasta, so the other ingredients do not suffer from longer reheating in the oven.

Lobster tails may be used, 1 large or 2 small lobster tails for 4 servings. If using raw lobster tails, cook for about half as much time as whole lobsters.

For an even more luxurious dish, substitute 200g/7oz fresh duck foie gras for the chicken livers. Slice and sauté quickly in a dry frying pan over high heat.

SOLE WITH TOMATO SAUCE

La sole au plat au coulis de tomates

SERVES 4

4 Dover soles, weighing 300g/10oz each
1kg/2lb ripe tomatoes
5 tbsp butter
3 shallots, peeled and chopped
bouquet garni
salt and pepper
parsley sprigs, to decorate

FOR THE FISH STOCK
200g/7oz white fish bones (eg, not salmon bones), including
the sole bones
3 tbsp butter
2 shallots, peeled and chopped
1 onion, peeled and chopped
parsley stems from 1 small bunch
4 tbsp white wine
2 litres/3 ¼ pints/8 cups water

Ask the fishmonger to skin and fillet the soles. Refrigerate the fillets until needed. Keep the heads and bones for making stock. To make the fish stock, wash any blood from the fish bones in cold running water. Melt the butter in a heavy saucepan over medium heat and sauté the bones until they are very lightly coloured, adding the shallots, onion and parsley stems. When the vegetables have softened, pour in the wine and the water. Let it bubble gently for 30 minutes, skimming off the foam that rises to the top from time to time. Strain the stock and remove any fat.

To make the tomato sauce, cut a shallow cross in the bottom of the tomatoes. Cover them with boiling water until the skin begins to peel back, then drain. Peel the tomatoes, cut them in half around the equator, squeeze out the seeds and chop the flesh. Melt 1 tbsp of the butter in a saucepan and sweat half of the shallots until softened. Add the tomatoes and the bouquet garni and cook gently, stirring frequently, until the tomatoes are soft and have lost about one quarter of their liquid. Purée in a food processor or food mill and season to taste.

To cook the fish, spread the remaining 4 tbsp of butter in large baking dish and sprinkle over the remaining shallots. Arrange the sole fillets in one layer, pour over the fish stock and cook in a preheated 220°C/425°F/gas mark 7 oven for about 12 minutes, or until the fish is opaque. Remove and drain the fillets.

To serve, divide the tomato sauce between 4 warmed plates, arrange the fillets on top and decorate with parsley sprigs.

Notes: As the stock in which the fish was cooked is not required for serving, it may be strained and used for another purpose. For a more concentrated flavour, simmer to reduce by about half or to taste.

Both the fish stock and the tomato sauce can be made earlier in the day. Refrigerate and reheat before use.

ROAST PIGEON
WITH GARLIC

Pigeonneaux farcis à l'ail

SERVES 4

4 pigeons, dressed and drawn weight about 350g/³/4lb each
6 garlic cloves
125g/¹/4lb firm white bread·(about 4 large slices)
6–7 tbsp milk
¹/2 tsp fresh thyme leaves or ¹/4 tsp dried thyme
salt and pepper
500g/1lb caul fat
2–4 tbsp butter
1 onion, chopped
1 carrot, chopped
bouquet garni
4 tbsp dry white wine
500ml/16 fl oz/2 cups game stock or chicken stock

ut off the wing tips and feet, if necessary, and remove any remaining feathers from the pigeons. To make the stuffing, crush 4 of the garlic cloves in a mortar with a pestle. After removing the crust, reduce the bread to crumbs by rubbing it through a sieve or tearing it finely with a fork. Add the breadcrumbs to the mortar and mash with the garlic, then add the milk a spoonful at a time to form a thick paste. Alternatively, drop the garlic cloves into a food processor while it is running. Scrape the sides of the workbowl, add the crustless bread in chunks and pulse until it is reduced to crumbs, and slowly pour the milk through the top until it is moistened. Add the thyme and season the stuffing highly with salt and pepper. Spoon one quarter of the stuffing in the cavity of each pigeon. Sprinkle the birds with salt and pepper. Wrap in caul fat and truss them.

Melt 2 tbsp of the butter in a roasting pan or cast-iron casserole and cook the onion and carrot with the remaining 2 garlic cloves, crushed, over medium heat until the onion is softened, about 5 minutes. Place the pigeons on their sides in the pan. Roast uncovered in a preheated 250°C/475°F/gas mark 9 oven for about 30 minutes, turning after 10 minutes to the other side, then turn breast side up for the last 10 minutes. Baste with the fat accumulated in the pan. Remove the cooked birds and keep warm.

To make the sauce, deglaze the roasting pan with the wine. Add the stock and boil to reduce by half. Strain the sauce and whisk in the remaining 2 tbsp of butter.

To serve, arrange the pigeons on a warmed serving platter or divide among 4 warmed plates. Pour a little of the sauce over the pigeons and pass the remainder separately.

Notes: The pigeons can be stuffed earlier in the day if both the stuffing and the birds are cold. Refrigerate until ½ hour before cooking.

If caul fat is not available, use 4 rashers (slices) bacon, streaky if possible. Place half a piece of bacon on each side of the breast and tie on.

VEGETABLE COMPOTE

Légumes en compote

SERVES 4

1 red pepper
3 tomatoes
1 bunch young carrots (about 10)
1 bunch small young turnips (about 10)
3 courgettes (zucchini)
6 tbsp butter
625g/1 1/4lb young peas, shelled (about 150g/5oz/1 cup
shelled peas)
125g/1/4 lb small pearl or pickling onions, peeled
salt and pepper
chervil, for garnishing

S crape the carrots lightly and cut off most of the greens, leaving about 2cm/3/4 inch. Peel the turnips and trim the greens in the same way. Slice the courgettes (zucchini) thickly. Melt 4 tbsp of the butter in a heavy saucepan and cook the carrots and turnips together very gently with 4 tbsp of water for 45 minutes, covered. After 15 minutes cooking time, add the courgettes (zucchini) and after 25 minutes, add the peas. Stir from time. to time, adding a little more water if the vegetables are in danger of cooking dry.

Grill (broil) the pepper or roast in a very hot oven until the skin is darkened and blistered. Enclose in a plastic bag until cool enough to handle. Peel off the skin,

cut in half and remove the core and seeds. Cut the flesh into thin strips and set aside.

Cut a shallow cross in the bottom of the tomatoes. Cover them with boiling water until the skin begins to peel back, then drain. Peel the tomatoes, cut them in half around the equator, squeeze out the seeds and chop the flesh. Set aside until needed.

Meanwhile, in another saucepan large enough to hold all the vegetables sauté the onions in the remaining 2 tbsp of butter until lightly coloured, then add the red pepper strips and 2 tbsp of water. Cook them covered, in the same manner as the other vegetables. After 30 minutes, add the chopped tomatoes with all the other vegetables and any remaining cooking liquid. Simmer for about 3 minutes longer to soften the tomato and season to taste. Serve garnished with sprigs of chervil.

Note: If thawed frozen peas are used, add at the end with the tomatoes.

CHOCOLATE
FONDANT CAKE

Fondant au chocolat

SERVES 6–8

500g/1lb good quality plain (semisweet) chocolate
500ml/16fl oz/2 cups whipping cream
1–2 tbsp cocoa powder, for sprinkling

Break the chocolate into very small pieces. Bring 125ml/4fl oz/½ cup of the cream to a full boil in a heavy saucepan. Add the chocolate pieces, and stir so that all the chocolate is submerged. Remove the pan from the heat and cover tightly. Let stand until the chocolate is completely melted and soft, about 15–20 minutes. Stir with a sturdy whisk for three minutes, during which time the texture will seem a bit grainy.

Whip the remainder of the cream with an electric beater. It should be firm and airy, but not completely stiff. Add the chocolate to the cream and fold it in with the beater on low speed. Pour the mixture into a 20cm/8 inch spring form mould or removeable-bottom cake pan lined with a circle of parchment or greaseproof paper. Chill for at least 4 hours or overnight.

To serve, remove the sides of the mould, invert a serving plate over the cake and turn them over together carefully. Pull off the paper and decorate the top with cocoa powder sprinkled through a sieve.

The legendary lore of France is rich. Nowhere does it better love to linger than around those Druidic remains which stud the north and west of France, and still hold the popular imaginations enthralled with their fresh and potent spell . . . These grey granite masses, huge, unhewn, misshapen, are scattered over many districts of France. Among the wild scenery of Brittany they seem in strange, unconscious harmony with surroundings as savage as themselves. Here all is in keeping; they are at home; their presence is appropriate.

R.E. PROTHERO *The Pleasant Land of France*

The month of June ushers in the Breton summer. Along with September, it is one of the most beautiful months in this sunny season. The tides of the equinox have washed away the uncertainty of spring, and everything seems to contribute to the pleasures of eating.

Now is the time for seafood at its peak. Oysters have mostly shed their soft roe and are gorged with the fresh water that flows through their beds. Fat blue lobsters are lured into traps. Schools of bass move nearer to the coast's brown rocks. And tangled seaweed, left to dry on the beach by the retreating tide, adds its briny odour to the fishing scene.

From the beaches and jetties, fishing lines are pulled taut in the hope of catching a wily bass or an unpredictable sole. Mended nets, traps and other fishing equipment are retrieved from trunks, ready for a new season.

The kitchen, too, moves into high gear for a rush of summer activity. The smells of broths simmered with aromatic vegetables and flavoured with iodine-rich shellfish waft through the air, keeping the appetite constantly whetted. It is the season of plenitude. All the ingredients are available to create memorable meals.

M E N U S

Oysters with Almonds and Garlic Butter
Les huîtres farcies aux amandes

Roast Lobster with Spiced Cream
Le homard rôti aux épices

Chicken Stuffed with Cheese and Chives
Le poulet au fromage blanc maigre et à la ciboulette

Carrot Flan with Chervil
Gâteau de carottes au cerfeuil

Tea Sorbet
Sorbet au thé

Minted Melon
Melon à la menthe et son coulis

Sea bass with Cream and Lemon
Blanquette de bar au citron

Roast Calves' Liver with Seaweed
Foie de veau rôti entier aux noris

Broccoli Timbales
Timbales de brocolis

Chocolate Mille-feuilles with Strawberries
Mille-feuilles de chocolat noir aux fraises

OYSTERS WITH ALMONDS AND GARLIC BUTTER

Les huîtres farcies aux amandes

SERVES 4

6 small cloves garlic, peeled
2 shallots, peeled
200g/7oz butter
4 tbsp chopped parsley
salt and pepper
25 oysters
1kg/2lb rock salt, for cooking
150g/5oz/1¼ cups sliced almonds

Make the garlic butter ahead, so it has time to chill. Mash the garlic and shallots in a mortar with a pestle. Mix in the butter and parsley, and season with a little salt and plenty of pepper. Alternatively, drop the garlic cloves into a food processor while it is running. Add the shallots and chop finely by pulsing the machine. Scrape the sides of the workbowl, add the butter, parsley and seasoning and mix well. Enclose the garlic butter in foil, forming a cylinder about 3cm/1¼ inches in diameter, and refrigerate at least 2 hours.

To open the oysters, hold in a cloth with the flat side up. Push an oyster knife into the hinge and around the edge to sever the muscle, which will allow the top shell to be pried off.

Pour the rock salt into a baking dish large enough to hold the oysters and settle them on the rock salt. Put a

thin slice of butter, about 3mm/⅛ inch, over each oyster and top with a pinch of sliced almonds. Any remaining butter can be used for another purpose. Grill (broil) the oysters under a preheated medium-hot grill (broiler) until the butter is bubbly and the almonds lightly browned, about 4 minutes. Arrange on 4 warmed plates and serve immediately.

Note: If necessary, the oysters may be cooked on a bed of crumpled foil instead of rock salt.

ROAST LOBSTER WITH SPICED CREAM

Le homard rôti aux épices

SERVES 4

4 live lobsters, weighing about 500g/1lb each
800ml/1⅓pt/3¼ cups whipping cream
1 tsp ground cardamom
1 tsp curry powder
1 tsp paprika
pinch cayenne pepper
125g/4oz/8 tbsp cold butter, cut in pieces

B ring a large pot of salted water to the boil. One at a time, plunge the lobsters into the water and cook for 2 minutes to kill them. Arrange the lobsters in a metal roasting pan and bake in a preheated 260°C/500°F oven for 10 minutes, then remove the lobsters and keep warm.

Heat the cream in a heavy saucepan with the spices and a pinch of salt. Boil gently until it is reduced by half. Add the reduced cream to the roasting pan and boil a few minutes, scraping the bottom of the pan to incorporate the lobster cooking juices. Whisk in the butter one piece at a time, then taste and adjust the seasoning, if needed. Strain the sauce and keep warm.

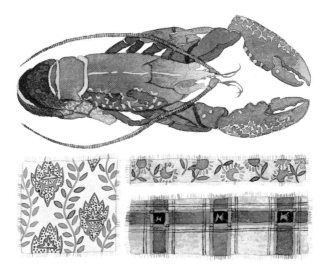

Cut the lobsters in half, holding firmly by the head right side up and inserting the point of a long heavy knife into the seam between the head and the body to cut down through the body and tail. Then hold the body and cut through the head in the same way. Remove the sack of 'gravel' behind the eyes and the intestinal thread from the tail. Crack the claws for easier serving. Place the halved lobsters cut side up on warmed serving plates and decorate with parsley sprigs. Pour over a little of the sauce and serve the rest separately.

Note: This recipe may be halved for 2 servings.

CHICKEN STUFFED
WITH CHEESE AND CHIVES

Le poulet au fromage blanc maigre et à la ciboulette

SERVES 4

1.5kg/3lb chicken, with giblets
salt and pepper
5 tbsp chopped chives
375g/¾lb low fat soft cheese
3 tbsp butter
150ml/5fl oz/⅔ cup chicken stock or water

Season the cavity of the chicken with salt and pepper. Mix the chives with the cheese and season with plenty of pepper and salt to taste. Stuff the chicken with the cheese mixture. Sew the openings firmly closed with a trussing needle.

Melt the butter in a cast-iron casserole over a moderate heat and add the giblets. Add the chicken and brown on all sides. When it is lightly coloured, add about half the stock or water, cover the casserole and transfer to a preheated 200°C/400°F/gas mark 6 oven.

Cook for about 45 minutes, basting with a few spoonfuls of the remaining stock or water from time to time, until the chicken is done and the juices run clear when the flesh is pierced with a skewer or the tip of a knife. Remove the chicken to a carving board and keep warm. Add any remaining stock to the casserole, boil gently for 2–3 minutes to reduce slightly and strain into a warmed sauceboat. Carve the chicken and serve with some of the cheese stuffing. Pass the sauce separately.

CARROT FLAN WITH CHERVIL

Gâteau de carottes au cerfeuil

SERVES 4–6

2kg/4lb large carrots
3 eggs
90ml/3fl oz/6 tbsp whipping cream
1 tbsp chopped chervil
1½ tsp sugar
salt and pepper

Peel the carrots and set aside 400g/¾lb, about 4 carrots. Slice the remaining carrots thickly and boil or steam until soft. Drain well and purée the carrot slices. If the purée seems watery, cook it in a non-stick saucepan over a moderate heat until some of the moisture is evaporated, stirring frequently. Allow the purée to cool.

Cut the reserved carrots into matchstick strips about 5cm/2 inches long and cook until tender.

Beat the eggs and cream together and mix with the carrot purée. Add the chervil and sugar, and season to taste with salt and pepper. Add the cooked carrot strips and transfer to a buttered ceramic tart or flan dish, or an oval gratin dish. Bake in a preheated 165°C/325°F/gas mark 3 oven for 20 minutes. Serve hot.

TEA SORBET

Sorbet au thé

SERVES 4

350g/12oz/1¾ cups sugar
450ml/15fl oz/scant 2 cups water
40g/1½oz/½ cup aromatic tea leaves
juice of ½ lemon
8 mint leaves

Put the sugar in a saucepan with the water and boil for 9 minutes. Turn off the heat, add the tea and cover the pan. Let it stand for about 2 hours or until completely cold. Stir in the lemon juice and strain the infusion into an ice cream machine. Freeze according to manufacturer's instructions.

To serve, spoon the sorbet into chilled bowls or glasses and decorate with mint leaves.

It was a hot blazing day; and, being very thirsty, we went into a farm-house to see if we could get some milk. We found the family very busy making crêpe; but were, nevertheless, received with the greatest hospitality. The peasants, almost invariably, prefer milk which has turned sour, and become curds and whey, to new milk. But they asked us which we would have, and, upon our requesting it fresh, brought forth two immense bowls, one for each of us; into which they were about to put, if we had not stopped them, a huge lump of butter, preparatory to boiling it. They were much surprised at our preferring it unturned, and butterless, and cold. The milk in Brittany is generally, I think, the richest I ever tasted.

T.A. TROLLOPE *A Summer in Brittany*

MINTED MELON

Melon à la menthe et son coulis

SERVES 4–6

*6 melons, each weighing about 500g/1lb, or 2 melons, each
weighing about 1.5kg/3lb
1 tbsp sugar
4 tbsp chopped mint leaves
lemon juice
20 raspberries, for garnishing
mint leaves, for garnishing*

Cut the melons in half and discard the seeds. Using a melon baller, cut three quarters of the melon flesh into balls. Scoop out any flesh left from between the balls and reserve. Cube the remaining melon flesh and purée it with the reserved trimmings in a food processor or food mill. Add the sugar, chopped mint, and lemon juice to taste.

Divide the melon balls among 4 chilled plates and pour over the melon purée. Garnish with raspberries and mint leaves.

SEA BASS WITH CREAM AND LEMON

Blanquette de bar au citron

SERVES 4

2 lemons, scrubbed and rinsed
1.5kg/3lb sea bass, scaled, filleted and skinned
2 tbsp chopped shallots
500ml/16fl oz/2 cups whipping cream
250ml/8fl oz/1 cup fish stock (see page 20) [Sole with Tomato Sauce]

Using a vegetable peeler, remove the zest (the yellow part of the peel) from the lemons. Cut into very thin julienne strips. Put in a small saucepan, cover with water and bring to a boil. Cook for 2 minutes, drain and reserve. Cut off the white pith from the lemons, then cut the fruit from between the membranes, removing the seeds. Set aside the lemon sections until needed.

Cut the sea bass fillets into 4 portions. Season with salt and pepper and arrange them in one layer in a buttered saucepan or flameproof casserole with the shallots. Add the cream and fish stock, bring to a boil, turn down the heat and simmer for 3–4 minutes, or until the flesh is opaque. Remove the fish with a slotted spoon and keep warm. Reduce the sauce by about one third. Taste and adjust the seasoning and strain the sauce.

Divide the fish among 4 warmed serving plates, spoon the sauce over and garnish with the lemon sections and julienne zest.

ROAST CALVES' LIVER
WITH SEAWEED

Foie de veau rôti entier aux noris

SERVES 4–6

350g/³⁄₄lb edible seaweed preserved in brine, or 30g/1oz dried
seaweed (nori, laver or sloke)
600g/1¹⁄₄lb calves' liver in 1 piece
salt and pepper
150g/5oz veal trimmings or veal stewing meat
7 tbsp butter
1 onion, chopped
1 garlic clove, crushed
2 tbsp dry white wine
125ml/4fl oz/¹⁄₂ cup water

If using preserved seaweed, rinse well and drain. If using dried seaweed, soak in cold water for at least 10 minutes to rehydrate, then rinse. Simmer rehydrated seaweed gently for about 5–10 minutes, depending on thickness, until tender, then drain.

Season the liver with salt and pepper. Cut the veal trimmings or stewing meat in fairly small pieces, about 2.5cm/1 inch. Melt 3 tbsp of the butter in a roasting pan or cast-iron casserole over a medium-high heat. Brown the pieces of veal. When they are lightly coloured, push them aside and add the liver. Brown quickly on all sides. Add the onion and garlic and transfer the pan to a

40

preheated 230°C/450°F/gas mark 8 oven. Roast for about 17 minutes for pink or 20 minutes for medium.

Remove the piece of calves' liver and keep warm. Deglaze the roasting pan with the wine and water, scraping the bottom of the pan to incorporate the brown bits. Boil gently for 5 minutes and strain the sauce. Heat the seaweed in the sauce, either in the roasting pan in the oven, covered, for 7 minutes or over moderate heat.

Carve the liver in slices, arrange on a warmed serving platter or individual plates, and garnish with the seaweed. Whisk the remaining butter into the sauce while boiling gently. Pour some sauce over the meat and serve the rest separately.

BROCCOLI TIMBALES

Timbales de brocolis

SERVES 6

1kg/2lb broccoli florets
4 tbsp butter
4 eggs
2 egg yolks
150ml/5fl oz/⅔ cup whipping cream
salt and pepper
grated nutmeg (optional)

enerously butter 6 custard cups or individual moulds with a capacity of 200ml/6fl oz/¾ cup each. For easier unmoulding, line the bases with buttered parchment or greaseproof paper. Alternatively, prepare a 1.25 litre/½ pint/5 cup ring mould or soufflé dish.

Cook the broccoli florets in boiling salted water until just barely tender or steam them. Refresh in cold water to stop the cooking and drain well.

Arrange about two thirds of the broccoli florets in the prepared moulds with the heads down, trimming off any stems that stick up. Purée these trimmings along with the surplus florets until smooth. Add the eggs, egg yolks and cream and mix well. Season highly with salt, pepper and a little grated nutmeg, if wished.

Fill the moulds with the broccoli custard mixture and set them in a shallow pan. Pour in boiling water to come half way up the sides of the moulds and bake in a preheated 175°C/350°F/gas mark 4 oven for 20 minutes for small moulds, or 25–35 minutes for larger moulds. To determine if they are done, a skewer inserted in the centre should come out moist but clean.

To serve, cut around the edge with a small knife and invert the flans on a serving platter or individual plates. Remove the paper if used.

CHOCOLATE MILLE-FEUILLES WITH STRAWBERRIES

Mille-feuilles de chocolat noir aux fraises

SERVES 4

600g/1½lb strawberries
150g/5oz/¾ cup sugar
1 tbsp powdered gelatine (unflavored gelatin) or 4 sheets of gelatine
250g/½lb good quality plain (semisweet) chocolate
1–2 tbsp each cocoa powder and icing (confectioner's) sugar, for sprinkling

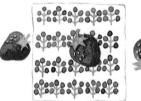

Wash the strawberries and remove the stems. Add the sugar and boil for 2 minutes. If using powdered gelatine, sprinkle it evenly over the surface of 2 tbsp of water in a small saucepan. Let stand for about 2 minutes or until the granules become translucent, then place the saucepan in a larger shallow pan of simmering water. Heat gently until the gelatine is completely dissolved, stirring occasionally. Add the liquid to the

44

strawberries. If using gelatine sheets, soak them in cold water until soft, squeeze out excess water and add to the strawberries.

Boil the strawberries for 2 minutes longer, stirring occasionally. The gelatine sheets, if used, will completely dissolve during this time. Cool the berries in a shallow dish in one layer and chill until needed.

Melt the chocolate over hot water in a bain-marie or in the top of a double-boiler. Cover a board at least 23×30cm/9×12 inches with foil. Using a metal spatula, spread the chocolate in a thin even layer. When the chocolate has begun to set, but is still fairly soft, cut through the chocolate to form 12 squares with 7cm/3 inch sides. Chill for 30 minutes, or until hardened. Remove the squares from the foil and return to the refrigerator until needed.

To assemble the mille-feuilles, place 4 squares of chocolate on a work surface. Divide half of the strawberries among them and top with 4 more squares of chocolate. Apportion the remaining strawberries and top with the remaining chocolate squares. Decorate the tops with cocoa powder and icing sugar sprinkled alternately through a sieve. Carefully transfer the mille-feuilles to chilled dessert plates.

Note: Handle the chocolate squares as quickly and gently as possible because they will begin to melt very rapidly from the heat of the hands.

A carpet of ochre has spread over the wooded hills. On the moors and embankments, the carpet is a green and grey one. The forests are deep brown and, out at sea, the waves are blue-green capped with lacy foam. These are the kaleidoscopic colours of a Breton September.

Autumn cooking picks up the same tones, with abundant hazelnuts, chestnuts, mushrooms and cider apples. These ingredients are paired with a vast assortment of feathered and furred game and served with a generous hand.

In nearby Muscadet, the grape harvest is already in, and the young wine, sampled with wild chestnuts, promises good things to come.

Partridge and hare are even now on our table, while the first frost will bring in woodcock. All this game profits from cooking with the plentiful wild cèpe and chanterelle mushrooms, smelling of woody bracken and dried grass.

The bounteous sea provides the first plump scallops and prawns – the ocean's harbingers of autumn, announcing the onset of rugged winter. Fishing poles and nets pull in countless varieties of seafood, including turbot, red snapper, lobster and cloudlike langoustine. Now is the time for gathering in the warmth of the kitchen.

M E N U S

Stuffed Mussels
Moules farcies

Steamed Scallops with Fennel and Leeks
Coquilles Saint Jacques en pot au feu à la vapeur de fenouil

Roast Partridge with Wild Mushrooms
Perdrix rôties aux chanterelles

Stuffed Cabbage Rolls
Choux farcis

Chestnut Cake with Hazelnut Custard Sauce
Le gâteau de marrons à la sauce noisette

Langoustines with Tarragon Butter Sauce
Langoustines grillées à l'estragon

Red Mullet Fillets with Diced Vegetables
Filets de rougets en 'barbouille'

Chicken with Apples and Cream
Fricassée de poulette aux pommes fruits

Artichokes with Bacon
Ragoût de fonds d'artichauts aux lardons

White Grape Iced Soufflé
Soufflé glacé au raisin blanc

STUFFED MUSSELS

Moules farcies

SERVES 4–6

4–5lb large mussels
500ml/16fl oz/2 cups Muscadet, or other dry white wine
2 tbsp finely chopped shallots
6 tbsp whipping cream
200g/7oz white bread (about 6–7 large slices)
2 tbsp finely chopped parsley
freshly ground white pepper
3 tbsp unsalted butter, cut in small pieces

Select large mussels for this recipe, about 12 to the pound. Scrub the mussels under cold running water, discarding any which are not firmly closed or do not close when tapped. Scrape off any loose barnacles and remove the tuft of 'beard' which may protrude from the edge of the shells. Put the mussels in a heavy saucepan or casserole, add the wine and cook covered over a high heat for 3–5 minutes until most of the mussels have opened. Remove the opened mussels with a slotted spoon and continue cooking those which may not have opened. Discard any which have not opened after 1–2 minutes further cooking.

Strain the cooking liquid into a saucepan through a sieve lined with muslin which has been rinsed and wrung dry. Add the chopped shallots and the cream. Bring to a boil and cook over a moderate heat until reduced by half; there should be about 300ml/10fl oz/1¼ cups.

After removing the crust, reduce the bread to crumbs by rubbing it through a sieve or tearing it finely with a fork. Stir the breadcrumbs into the cooking liquid with the butter and mix until thickened. Add the parsley and season with pepper; salt will not be necessary. Alternatively, chop the bread into crumbs in a food processor, pour in the reduced cooking liquid and mix, adding the parsley, pepper and butter at the end. Cool the stuffing.

Remove half of each shell, leaving the flesh attached to the remaining half. Spread some stuffing over each mussel and arrange them in a large baking dish. Brown the mussels under a preheated hot grill (broiler) until bubbly and nicely coloured, about 3–4 minutes. Serve immediately on warmed plates.

STEAMED SCALLOPS
WITH FENNEL AND LEEKS

*Coquilles Saint Jacques en pot au feu à la
vapeur de fenouil*

SERVES 4

*2 leeks
1 large fennel bulb
1 litre/1²/₃ pints/4 cups water
16 large sea scallops
salt and pepper
3 carrots, peeled and coarsely chopped
1 celery stalk, coarsely chopped
2 garlic cloves, peeled and crushed
200g/7oz cold butter, cut in pieces
juice of ½ lemon*

Cut the white part of the leeks into thin julienne or matchstick strips and coarsely chop the greens. Slice the base off the fennel bulb and remove three outer layers. Trim off the tops and slice the pieces of fennel vertically into thin julienne or matchstick strips. Reserve these with the strips of leek. Chop the remainder of the fennel bulb and put it with the leek greens, carrots, celery and garlic cloves in the bottom part of a steamer. Add the water, cover and boil gently for 10 minutes.

Remove the scallops from the shells, if necessary. Detach the coral and reserve for another purpose.

Season the scallops generously with salt and pepper and put them in the top part of the steamer. Arrange the strips of fennel and leek over them, cover tightly and steam for 10 minutes.

Meanwhile, put the butter and lemon juice in a small saucepan with 2 tbsp of water and boil very gently for 3–4 minutes until it is well blended and smooth. If the sauce has not thickened, use a hand blender to emulsify it and give it a creamy texture. Taste and season the sauce before serving.

Serve the scallops and julienne vegetables directly from the steamer and pass the sauce separately.

ROAST PARTRIDGE WITH WILD MUSHROOMS

Perdrix rôties aux chanterelles

SERVES 4

4 young partridges, dressed and drawn
salt and pepper
250g/½lb butter (approximate)
4 slices firm white bread, crusts removed
350g/¾lb chanterelles or girolles, washed and stemmed
3 tbsp Armagnac
8 tbsp whipping cream
1 bunch watercress

Preheat the oven to 250°C/480°F/gas mark 10. Season the partridges inside and out with salt and pepper. Put 1 tbsp of the butter inside each bird and smear the skin generously with more butter. Roast the birds for 20 minutes, basting twice with the pan drippings or if necessary with additional butter.

Meanwhile, cut the bread diagonally to make 8 croûtons. Melt 3 tbsp of butter and fry them over a moderate heat until browned. Keep them warm.

Melt 3 tbsp of butter and sauté the mushrooms, stirring occasionally as they cook. Season to taste with salt and pepper.

After 20 minutes' roasting, check that the partridges are done. Insert a trussing needle into the breast and remove: the drops of liquid which run out should be clear. Large birds may need a few minutes longer. Remove the cooked birds and keep warm. Pour off the accumulated fat and deglaze the roasting pan with the Armagnac. Flame it, and when the flames die out, add the cream. Scrape the bottom of the roasting pan to incorporate the browned bits. Boil to reduce slightly, then whisk in 2 tbsp cold butter. Taste and adjust the seasoning if necessary.

Arrange the croûtons on 4 warmed plates. Cut the partridges in half, place each cut side down on a croûton and garnish with sautéed chanterelles and bouquets of watercress. Strain the sauce into a sauceboat, coat the birds with a little sauce and pass the remainder.

Notes: If chanterelles are not available use other wild mushrooms or flavourful cultivated mushrooms.

STUFFED CABBAGE ROLLS

Choux farcis

SERVES 4

1 or 2 heads loose-leaved green cabbage
125g/¼lb veal stewing meat, cut in cubes
125g/¼lb fatty pork, cut in cubes
4 tbsp snipped chives
salt and pepper
ground allspice or quatre-épices
nutmeg
125g/¼lb pork rind
1 onion, peeled and chopped
1 carrot, peeled and thinly sliced
2 garlic cloves, peeled and thinly sliced
2–3 tbsp butter
4 tbsp Muscadet, or other dry white wine
600ml/1 pint/2½ cups chicken stock

emove 20 large cabbage leaves without tearing them. Wash them and cut out the thick main stem. Blanch them 3 or 4 at a time in boiling salted water for about 2 minutes until they become bright green and limp. Drain on clean tea towels.

To make the stuffing using a food processor, coarsely chop 100g/3½oz of the remaining cabbage (about 1½ cups, chopped). Add the veal and pork and chop, using a pulsing motion so the mixture does not become puréed. Add the chives and season well with salt and pepper, a

pinch of ground allspice or quatre-épices and a little freshly grated nutmeg. Alternatively, use a meat grinder or chop the stuffing ingredients very finely by hand.

Spread the cabbage leaves out on a work surface. Divide the filling among the leaves, placing a rounded tablespoonful of stuffing at the tip of each leaf. Roll up, tucking in the edges of the leaves to make a tidy package.

Put the pork rind, onion, carrot and garlic in the bottom of a buttered flameproof baking dish or casserole. Arrange the cabbage rolls on top and pour over the wine and stock. Bring to a boil, cover and put in a preheated 250°C/480°F oven for 35 minutes.

Remove the cabbage rolls and reduce the cooking liquid by three quarters. Taste and adjust the seasoning if necessary.

Notes: Savoy cabbage or the large leaves of spring greens are easy to handle. If it is difficult to remove the leaves from a round-heart cabbage, blanch the whole head in boiling water before removing the leaves.

Bacon may be substituted for the pork rind. If fresh chives are not available, use 3 tbsp finely chopped spring onions or scallions.

CHESTNUT CAKE WITH HAZELNUT CUSTARD SAUCE

Le gâteau de marrons à la sauce noisette

SERVES 4–6

150g/5oz plain (semisweet) chocolate, broken in small pieces
3 tbsp butter, cut in pieces
500g/1lb unsweetened canned chestnut purée
100g/3½oz/¾ cup icing (confectioner's) sugar

FOR THE SAUCE

500ml/16fl oz/2 cups milk
90g/3oz/⅔ cup chopped hazelnuts
6 egg yolks
100g/3½oz/½ cup sugar

repare the cake 2 days before serving. Line a glass or ceramic terrine, having a capacity of 1 litre/1⅔ pints/4 cups, with parchment or greaseproof paper.

Melt the chocolate and butter in a saucepan over hot water in a bain-marie or in the top of a double-boiler.

Meanwhile, beat the chestnut purée with the icing (confectioner's) sugar in a large bowl, using an electric mixer or a sturdy whisk. When the chocolate and butter have melted, add to the sweetened chestnut purée and beat the two mixtures together vigorously until soft and fluffy, trying to incorporate as much air as possible.

Pour the mixture into the prepared terrine and chill in the coldest part of the refrigerator for 48 hours.

To make the sauce, bring the milk to a boil in a heavy-bottomed saucepan with the hazelnuts.

Meanwhile, beat the egg yolks and sugar until pale and fluffy, about 3–4 minutes. Pour the hot milk over the egg mixture while whisking vigorously, then pour it all back into the saucepan. Cook over moderate heat, stirring constantly, until the custard has thickened and will coat the back of a spoon, about 15 minutes. To test, remove the spoon from the custard sauce and, using a finger, draw a line across the back: it should remain and not be filled in. Remove from the heat, strain the sauce and allow to cool. Discard the hazelnuts. Chill the sauce.

To serve, unmould the chestnut cake and cut into slices. Arrange on the plates and surround with hazelnut custard sauce.

Note: If prepared hazelnuts are not available, toast shelled nuts in a preheated 200°C/400°F/gas mark 6 oven for 5 minutes, put them into a clean tea towel and rub briskly to remove the skins, then chop.

L A N G O U S T I N E S   W I T H
T A R R A G O N   B U T T E R
S A U C E

Langoustines grillées à l'estragon

SERVES 4

3 ripe tomatoes
2 tbsp olive oil
16 langoustines (Dublin Bay prawns), about 180g/6oz each
6 tbsp melted butter
salt and pepper
200g/7oz cold butter, cut in pieces
juice of ½ lemon
1½ tbsp chopped fresh tarragon

To peel the tomatoes, cut a shallow cross in the base, remove the stem and cover them with boiling water for about 30 seconds or until the skin begins to roll back. Drain, peel and cut them in half crossways. Squeeze out the seeds and dice the flesh into small cubes, about 3mm/⅛ inch. Marinate them with the olive oil in a small bowl.

Preheat the oven to 280°C/525°F or the highest setting. Split the langoustines in half lengthwise with a sturdy knife or cleaver. Arrange the shellfish cut side up in a large shallow baking dish, brush with melted butter and season them with salt and pepper. Bake at the top of the preheated oven for 10 minutes.

Meanwhile, put the cold butter and lemon juice with 1 tbsp of water in a small saucepan and boil very gently for 3–4 minutes until it is well blended and smooth. If the sauce has not thickened, use a hand blender to emulsify it and give it a creamy texture. Add the tarragon and season to taste.

Arrange the langoustines on warmed plates, put a little chopped tomato on each, particularly on the heads, and pass the sauce.

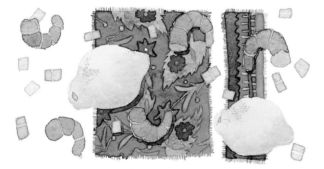

Notes: If preferred, remove the heads before splitting the tails. The heads may be used for shellfish sauce or stock. Langoustines are quite perishable and if they are only available already cooked, they will do for this recipe, but decrease the cooking time by 2–3 minutes.

RED MULLET FILLETS WITH DICED VEGETABLES

Filets de rougets en 'barbouille'

SERVES 4

4 red mullet, about 300g/10oz each
2 courgettes (zucchini)
2–3 tbsp olive oil
2 tomatoes
2 lemons
350ml/11fl oz/1 ⅓ cups fish stock (see page 20) [Sole with
Tomato Sauce]
150g/5oz/10 tbsp butter
salt and pepper
20 chives, cut in 5cm/2 inch lengths, for garnishing

Ask the fishmonger to scale and fillet the red mullet. Remove any fine bones remaining with tweezers.

Wash the courgettes (zucchini), and cut them into small cubes, about 3mm/⅛ inch square. Heat the olive oil and fry them over fairly high heat until lightly browned, stirring frequently. Drain on paper towels.

Cut a shallow cross in the bottom of the tomatoes, remove the core and cover them with boiling water for about 30 seconds. Drain, peel and cut them in half crossways. Squeeze out the seeds and dice the flesh into

small cubes, about 3mm/⅛ inch. Peel the lemons, leaving no white pith, and carefully slice the fruit from between the membranes. Cut the lemon sections into small pieces and reserve with the diced tomato.

Reduce the fish stock by half and whisk in 60g/2oz/ 4 tbsp butter. Add the diced vegetables and lemon. Season the sauce with salt and pepper.

Melt the remaining butter, brush the fish fillets generously and season them. Fry them over a moderately high heat for about 2 minutes on each side, starting skin side up.

Arrange the cooked fillets on warmed plates and spoon out the pieces of vegetables and fruit from the sauce, dividing them evenly. Pour a spoonful of liquid over each plate and pass the remainder of the sauce. Serve immediately, garnished with chives.

Note: Red snapper may be used in place of red mullet.

CHICKEN WITH APPLES AND CREAM

Fricassée de poulette aux pommes fruits

SERVES 4

1.75kg/4lb chicken
salt and pepper
6 tbsp melted butter
3 tbsp chopped shallots
4 apples, peeled and cored
2 tbsp calvados or applejack
350ml/11fl oz/1⅓ cups whipping cream

C ut the chicken into 8 pieces and season with salt and pepper. Brown them slowly in 1 tbsp of the butter in a heavy cast-iron casserole. If the pieces will not fit in one layer, brown them in batches. When all are nicely coloured, pour off the fat and add the shallots. Cover the casserole and cook over a very low heat for 20 minutes, checking from time to time to make sure it doesn't burn on the bottom. If necessary, add 1–2 tbsp water.

Meanwhile, cut the apples into eighths. Toss them in the remaining melted butter until well covered. Arrange the pieces of apple on a baking tray and cook in a preheated 220°C/425°F/gas mark 7 oven for about 15 minutes, or until the edges are browned.

After 20 minutes' cooking, add the calvados and cream to the casserole with the chicken and simmer for 10 minutes. Remove the chicken from the casserole and keep warm. Remove the shallots with a slotted spoon and discard. Reduce the cream to thicken it a little. Taste and adjust the seasoning and pour the sauce into a warmed sauce boat.

Arrange the chicken on 4 warmed plates or a serving platter. Garnish with the apples and nap with a little of the sauce. Serve the remaining sauce separately.

Notes: Chicken pieces may be used, about 1.5kg/3½lb. If all white meat is used, reduce the time by 5 minutes.

For easier clean-up, line the baking tray with foil before cooking the apples.

ARTICHOKE BOTTOMS
WITH BACON

Ragoût de fonds d'artichauts aux lardons

SERVES 4

6 large artichokes
200g/7oz thick sliced streaky bacon, cut into thin strips
200ml/7fl oz chicken stock
4 tbsp cold unsalted butter, cut in pieces
4 tbsp snipped chives

Trim the stems flat with the bottom and cook the artichokes in boiling salted water until the bottom is tender, about 35–40 minutes. Pull off the leaves and scoop out the fuzzy centre part or the 'choke'. Keep the artichoke bottoms warm until needed.

Meanwhile fry the bacon pieces over a moderate heat until crisp, stirring frequently for even browning. Drain on paper towels.

Reduce the chicken stock by two thirds. Whisk in the butter one piece at a time and add the chives.

Slice the artichoke bottoms and arrange on warmed serving plates. Pour about 1½ tbsp of sauce over each and garnish with bacon.

Notes: The artichokes may be cooked ahead of time and reheated in the stock. Remove and keep warm while finishing the sauce.

W H I T E   G R A P E   I C E D   S O U F F L E

Soufflé glacé au raisin blanc

SERVES 4–6

700g/1½lb white grapes (seedless, if possible)
sugar
2 egg whites, at room temperature
2–3 tbsp biscuit (cookie) crumbs

This recipe must be made at least 5 hours in advance. Chill a 1 litre/1⅔ pint/4 cup soufflé dish or 6 individual soufflé dishes.

Rinse the grapes and blot dry in a thick towel. If they are not seedless, halve them and remove the seeds. Purée them in a food processor, and strain to remove the skins, pushing through as much pulp as possible. Alternatively, pass the grapes through a rotary food mill.

Weigh the grape pulp and juice, then weigh out one third that weight in sugar and remove 100g/3½oz/½ cup for the meringue. Add the remaining sugar to the grape pulp and juice and stir until dissolved. Put the mixture into an ice cream freezer and freeze according to manufacturer's instructions until soft. It should not be frozen solid before adding the meringue.

Meanwhile make the syrup for the meringue. Put the reserved sugar in a small heavy saucepan with 50ml/2fl oz/¼ cup water and bring to a boil. Boil until it reaches the hard-ball stage (125°C/250°F on a candy thermometer) and the surface is covered with large even bubbles, about 6–8 minutes. After the sugar has started to boil, begin beating the egg whites, slowly at first, then increasing the speed. The egg whites should stand in soft peaks when the sugar syrup is ready. Pour the sugar over the whites in a thin stream while turning the bowl at the same time. For this it is useful to have a mixer on a stand or, if using a hand mixer or whisk, the help of another person. Do not allow the sugar syrup to cook beyond this stage or it will form hard pieces in the meringue. After the syrup is added, continue beating for several minutes until the meringue is thick and shiny. Cool the meringue (set the bowl in a pan of ice water and continue beating, if time is short) and fold it into the partially frozen grape mixture in the ice cream machine. Let the machine run for 15 minutes longer.

Secure a paper collar to extend 3cm/1½ inches beyond the top of the soufflé mould and fill with the iced soufflé mixture. Sprinkle the crumbs on top and store in the freezer for at least 2 hours. Remove the collar before serving.

Notes: If you can only measure the sugar by volume (cups), it will be a bit less than one quarter the volume of the grape pulp and juice.

Instead of crumbs, the soufflé(s) may be decorated just before serving with halved grapes arranged cut side down and mint leaves.

A semi-circular bowl of granite slabs in broken tiers, with tall dark ranks of pine trees and autumn-tinted chestnuts rising one above the other among their irregular steps, composed a vast natural amphitheatre. Into it the wintry sun was pouring pale colour rather than diffusing light, and autumn had spread its tawny carpet of dead leaves over all. At the centre of this chamber, which appeared to have had the Flood for architect, rose three enormous Druidic stones.

HONORÉ DE BALZAC *Les Chouans*

The Breton winter is very mild. Snow and frost are rare. It is a quiet season, too, except on stormy days when the wind from the west chases the sea gulls inland and makes the waves curl in a crest of foam along the shore. In weather like this, it's out of the question to go out to sea. Only the oyster parks are accessible, and this is the oyster's best season.

Food is more rooted in the land at this time of the year, and a cook's creativity is put to the test. The autumn vegetables are still available and winter ones are just coming in, as well as winter fruits.

This is the time for delving into traditional, regional cooking, for rediscovering the gastronomic past and preparing old favourites such as crêpes, galettes and hearty *fars*.

On days when the sea is calm sea urchins can be found, to flavour dishes with their iodine-rich, perfumed taste.

It is the season of short days and long meals, the season of fires in the hearth and shutters pulled tight against the blustery wind.

MENUS

Hot Crab Soufflé
Le soufflé chaud de crabe

Salmon with Seaweed and Foie Gras
Carpaccio de saumon, algues laminaires et foie gras chaud

Pork with Cockles
Filet de porc aux coques caramélisées

Cucumber Gratin
Gratin de concombre

Breton Prune Flan
Far breton aux pruneaux

Monkfish with Sea Urchin Sauce
Piccata de lotte au corail d'oursins

Sole Fillets with Pineapple
Filets de sole rôtie à l'ananas

Steak with Anchovy Butter Sauce
Pièce de boeuf beurre rouge aux anchois

Truffled Chestnuts
Ragoût de châtaignes truffé

Apple Crêpes
Crêpes aux pommes

HOT CRAB SOUFFLE

Le soufflé chaud de crabe

SERVES 4–6

4 large crabs, about 600g/1¼lb each
200ml/6fl oz/¾ cup whipping cream
¾ tsp corn flour (cornstarch)
salt and pepper
3 egg whites

Several hours ahead or the day before, cook the crabs in boiling salted water for 10 minutes. When they are cool enough to handle easily, pull off the claws and legs. Separate the body from the shell and remove the meat and the coral from the body. Scoop out the meat from the shell. (This darker crabmeat gives body and flavour to the soufflés.) There should be approximately 750g/1 ½lb/3 cups of crabmeat.

Crack the claws, remove the meat and pick over it carefully with the fingers to remove any pieces of shell. Reserve the claw meat separately. Scrub the shells and cut into the seam on the underside of the shell with scissors. The inner part of the shell should break off along the seam, enlarging the opening. Rinse and dry the shells well.

To make the soufflés, purée the body crabmeat in a food processor and push through a sieve to remove small bits of shell. Mix the cream with the corn flour

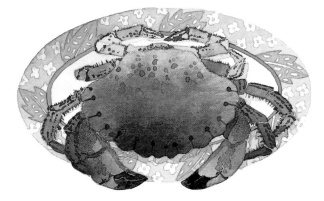

(cornstarch) and stir into the puréed crabmeat. Add the reserved claw meat. Season with a little salt and a generous amount of pepper.

Beat the egg whites with a pinch of salt until they form stiff peaks. Fold a spoonful into the crab mixture to lighten it. Then quickly and gently fold the crab mixture into the egg whites. Spoon the soufflé mixture into the crab shells, mounding it up. Alternatively, spoon the mixture into buttered individual soufflé dishes. It will fill 4 large or 6 medium-large individual dishes.

Put the prepared soufflés on a baking tray and bake in a preheated 200°C/400°F/gas mark 6 oven for 15 minutes. Serve immediately.

SALMON WITH SEAWEED AND FOIE GRAS

Carpaccio de saumon, algues laminaires et foie gras chaud

SERVES 4

3 tbsp Balsamic or malt vinegar
6 tbsp olive oil
salt and pepper
800g/1¾lb skinless salmon fillet
100g/3½oz edible seaweed preserved in brine, or 7g/¼oz dried seaweed
300g/10oz fresh foie gras
1 tbsp pink peppercorns in brine, drained

P ut the vinegar into a small bowl, whisk in the olive oil and season with salt and pepper. Cut the salmon in very thin slices, holding the knife almost parallel with the fillet. There should be 16 slices. Arrange on a large platter, in one layer if possible, cover evenly with the vinaigrette dressing and marinate about 1 hour.

If using preserved seaweed, drain well. If using dried seaweed, soak in cold water for at least 10 minutes to rehydrate, rinse and drain. Cut the seaweed across the leaves into very thin ribbons. If the seaweed is not tender, simmer for about 5–10 minutes, depending on thickness, until tender, then drain.

Slice the foie gras into 12 pieces about 6mm/¼ inch thick and season them with salt and pepper. Preheat a heavy frying pan over a high heat. Dry-fry the slices quickly so as not to melt them. Drain on paper towels.

To serve, arrange the marinated salmon on 4 plates, garnish with seaweed and pink peppercorns and arrange the hot slices of sautéed foie gras around the edge.

PORK WITH COCKLES

Filet de porc aux coques caramélisées

SERVES 4

500g/1lb cockles
2 pork fillets (tenderloins), about 900g/1¾lb total weight
125ml/4fl oz/½ cup dry white wine
salt and pepper
6 tbsp sugar
60g/2oz/4 tbsp butter
3 shallots, peeled and quartered
7 tbsp water
½ tsp soy sauce

Rinse the cockles in two changes of water. Put them in a heavy saucepan or cast-iron casserole with the wine, cover tightly, and steam them open over high heat. Remove the cockles from the shells. Strain the cooking liquid into a small saucepan through a sieve lined with muslin which has been rinsed and wrung dry. Add the sugar and boil gently until the mixture is reduced by about half and has thickened slightly. Keep the cockles warm in this syrup.

Remove any fat or membrane from the outside of the pork and season with salt and pepper.

Melt half of the butter in a heavy frying pan and cook the pork fillets over a moderate heat, turning frequently for even browning. Remove and keep warm when done, after about 15 minutes. Add the shallots to the same pan and cook until they are lightly browned. Add the water, scrape the bottom of the pan to dissolve the browned bits, and boil gently to reduce the sauce by about one quarter. Whisk in the remaining butter and the soy sauce.

Carve the pork into slices about 1cm/³⁄₈ inch thick and divide them among 4 warmed plates, arranging the slices in a circle. Spoon the cockles into the middle of the circles. Garnish with the shallots. Add any carving juices to the sauce, along with the syrup from the cockles. Taste and adjust the seasoning, adding a little more soy sauce if wished. Serve the sauce in a warmed sauce boat.

Note: If cockles are not available, substitute small clams.

CUCUMBER GRATIN

Gratin de concombre

SERVES 4

3 cucumbers
2 tbsp coarse salt
150ml/5fl oz/⅔ cup whipping cream
freshly ground pepper
grated nutmeg
5 tbsp unsalted butter
100g/3½oz/1 cup grated Gruyère or Swiss cheese (optional)

Peel the cucumbers and split them lengthwise. Using a small spoon, scoop out the seeds and cut the cucumbers into 1cm/⅜ inch slices. Put them in a colander, sprinkle with salt and let stand for 2 hours to render some of their water. Rinse the cucumber slices and pat dry. Simmer them in cream over low heat for 15 minutes, stirring frequently. Season with pepper and nutmeg; salt will not be necessary.

Remove the cucumber slices from the cream with a slotted spoon and transfer them to a generously buttered shallow baking dish or gratin dish. Dot the remainder of the butter over the top, sprinkle with cheese, if wished, and brown the top under a preheated hot grill (broiler). Serve immediately.

Note: Be careful not to boil the cream or it can curdle. It is not used for the final stage of cooking.

BRETON PRUNE FLAN

Far breton aux pruneaux

SERVES 4–6

750ml/1¼ pints/3 cups milk
1 vanilla pod
butter, for the baking dish
180g/6oz pitted prunes
4 tbsp flour
100g/3½oz/½ cup sugar
4 eggs
1 tbsp rum
4 tbsp melted butter
icing (confectioner's) sugar, for sprinkling

P ut the milk in a heavy saucepan with the vanilla pod, split lengthways. Bring the milk to a boil, remove from the heat and allow it to cool to room temperature. Scrape the seeds from the vanilla pod and stir them into the milk.

Preheat the oven to 220°C/425°F/gas mark 7. Generously butter a round or oval shallow porcelain baking dish. Arrange the prunes in the dish.

Combine the flour and sugar in a deep mixing bowl. Break the eggs into the milk and whisk together. Whisk the milk and egg mixture into the dry ingredients. Mix quickly and do not overbeat. Strain the batter and stir in the rum and melted butter.

Pour the batter into the prepared dish and bake for about 30 minutes, watching it carefully to achieve a uniformly light brown colour and to prevent overbrowning. Let it cool in the baking dish and sprinkle icing (confectioner's) sugar through a sieve over the top. Cut into wedges to serve.

Note: If the prunes are hard, soak them in hot water for 30 minutes and drain before using.

The atmosphere of the little Breton town was one of total seclusion, almost stifling calm. It felt as if it was miles inland. Then suddenly, as we arrived in the church square, we were surrounded by dazzling light, an almighty blast of fresh air and the tremendous roar of the sea. It was the Ocean, the immense, boundless Ocean, with its fresh salty smell and the great gusts released by the rising tide with every boisterous wave.

ALPHONSE DAUDET *Contes du Lundi*

MONKFISH WITH SEA URCHIN SAUCE

Piccata de lotte au corail d'oursins

SERVES 4

900g/2lb monkfish tail
8 sea urchins, plus 8 more for garnishing, if wished
salt and pepper
5 large carrots
4 large white turnips
125g/4oz butter
150ml/5fl oz/⅔ cup fish stock (see page 20) [Sole with
Tomato Sauce]

emove any skin or membrane from the monkfish and fillet it, or ask the fishmonger to do it.

To open the sea urchins, hold in a towel with the concave side up and cut around the 'button' or mouth with poultry shears or scissors. Do not insert the scissors under the mouth, but cut around it to free that part from the rest of the shell. Enlarge the opening by cutting away most of the top. Remove the mouth and the inedible guts will come with it. Pour the liquid from 8 sea urchins through a fine strainer and reserve for the sauce. Scoop out the five orange parts and leave behind the brown part, as only the coral is eaten.

Peel the carrots and turnips and cut them into small ovals with a special root vegetable cutter or use a melon baller. If preferred, cut the vegetables into sticks. Boil the vegetables in salted water or steam them until just tender.

Cut the monkfish into slices about 2cm/¾ inch thick, and season with salt and pepper. Melt half of the butter in a heavy saucepan or cast-iron casserole over a moderately high heat. When the butter begins to foam, add the fish and sauté about 2 minutes, turning the pieces. Remove with a slotted spoon and keep warm. Add the fish stock and the reserved sea urchin liquid, scraping the bottom of the pan to incorporate the brown bits. Boil to reduce by half.

Meanwhile, blend together the coral from 8 sea urchins with the remaining butter. Whisk the mixture into the reduced liquid, and strain the sauce. Reheat the vegetables in a little butter and season to taste.

Arrange the pieces of fish on warmed serving plates, nap with the sauce and garnish with the additional sea urchin coral, if using, and the vegetables. Serve immediately.

Note: Special scissors for opening sea urchins are recommended, if available. Allow plenty of time to open them as this can be a lengthy process.

SOLE FILLETS WITH PINEAPPLE

Filets de sole rôtie à l'ananas

SERVES 4

4 Dover soles, each weighing about 400g/14oz
1 small pineapple, about 300g/10oz
1 lemon
5 tbsp sugar
salt and pepper
180g/6oz butter, melted
parsley, to decorate

Ask the fishmonger to skin and fillet the soles. Peel the pineapple and remove any brown spots and the fibrous core. Cut the pineapple into triangular pieces about 1cm/⅜ inch thick and 4cm/1½ inches per side. Heat the juice of half the lemon in a heavy saucepan with the sugar and 375ml/12fl oz/1½ cups of water. Add the pineapple pieces and simmer for 12 minutes. Remove the fruit and reduce the cooking liquid until it reaches a syrupy consistency.

Season the fish fillets with salt and pepper. Brush a large ovenproof baking dish with melted butter and arrange the sole fillets in one layer. Brush the top surface of the fish with butter and bake them in a preheated 220°C/425°F/gas mark 7 oven for about 15 minutes, basting twice. When the soles are cooked, remove and keep warm. Strain the cooking butter into the syrup, reheat and season with lemon juice, salt and pepper.

To serve, arrange the fish on warmed plates, pour over some of the pineapple butter sauce, garnish with pineapple pieces and decorate with sprigs of parsley.

Notes: If preferred, use 1 large Dover sole, weighing 1kg/2¼lb, and increase cooking time by 3–4 minutes. The larger sole may be cooked whole, without skin, and filleted after cooking, but it will need 5–10 minutes more cooking time.

If lemon sole fillets are substituted, decrease basic cooking time by 2–3 minutes.

STEAK WITH ANCHOVY
BUTTER SAUCE

Pièce de boeuf beurre rouge aux anchois

SERVES 4

180g/6oz butter
125g/¼lb shallots, peeled and chopped
500ml/16fl oz/2 cups red burgundy, or other red wine
bouquet garni
4 anchovies, plus more for garnishing
2 tbsp peppercorns
2 tsp coarse salt
4 boneless steaks, about 250g/½lb each (sirloin strip,
entrecôte or rib steaks)

Cut 125g/4oz of the butter into small pieces and chill until needed. Melt one quarter of the remaining butter in a heavy saucepan over medium heat. Add the shallots and cook for 3–4 minutes, stirring occasionally. Add the wine and bouquet garni and boil gently until only about 3 tbsp of liquid are left.

Rinse the anchovies and blot dry. Mash them to a paste and mix with the remaining butter.

Crush the peppercorns under the bottom of a heavy saucepan or with a mallet. Mix the crushed pepper with the coarse salt and press into the surface of the meat.

When the wine has reduced, add the reserved 8 tbsp butter, 1 or 2 pieces at a time, whisking constantly over a

moderate heat. The sauce should bubble gently, but it is useful to remove the pan from the heat from time to time while whisking, to keep the butter from melting too quickly, which may cause the sauce to break. Whisk in the anchovy butter last, then strain the sauce and keep warm in a water bath or a barely warm oven until serving.

Cook the steaks under a preheated hot grill (broiler) or pan fry quickly over high heat until cooked to the desired degree.

To serve, slice the meat, arrange on warmed plates, surround with a little sauce and garnish with whole anchovies. Pass the remaining sauce separately.

Note: Two or three steaks, weighing a total of 2lb, may be used in this recipe.

TRUFFLED CHESTNUTS

Ragoût de châtaignes truffé

SERVES 4

600g/1¼ lb chestnuts
500ml/16fl oz/2 cups milk
salt and pepper
5 tbsp butter
75g/2½oz fresh truffle, or 1 canned truffle, thinly sliced

Cut a cross through base of the shell of the chestnuts and blanch them in rapidly boiling water for 2 minutes. As soon as they are cool enough to handle, remove the outer shell and the inner skin. Bring the milk to a boil in a heavy saucepan with a little salt and pepper. Add the chestnuts, reduce the heat and simmer for 20 minutes. Remove the chestnuts from the milk, transfer to a warmed serving dish and keep warm.

Reduce the milk by about one third. Purée the bits of chestnut remaining in the milk, which will have thickened from the flour in the chestnuts. Whisk in the butter in pieces and adjust the seasoning if necessary. Pour the sauce over the chestnuts and garnish with truffle slices.

Notes: If using vacuum-packed or canned chestnuts (about 500g/1lb), reduce the cooking time by 5 minutes.

For maximum truffle flavour, put the truffle slices in the milk to infuse. Leave them in while the milk comes to the boil, then remove before adding the chestnuts.

APPLE CREPES

Crêpes aux pommes

SERVES 4

1kg/2¼lb apples, preferably golden delicious
6 tbsp melted butter, plus more for cooking the crêpes
60g/2oz/⅓ cup caster (granulated) sugar
icing (confectioner's) sugar, for sprinkling

FOR THE CREPES

250g/½lb/2 cups flour
pinch salt
2 tsp sugar
3 large eggs
500ml/16fl oz/2 cups milk
grated zest of 1 lemon

Make the crêpe batter about 2 hours in advance. Put the flour, salt, sugar and eggs into a bowl. Slowly pour in the milk, whisking constantly. Strain the batter, add the grated lemon zest and set aside for 2 hours. The batter thickens on standing, so it may be necessary to add a little water before cooking the crêpes; the batter should be the consistency of pouring custard (custard sauce).

To cook the crêpes, brush a crêpe pan or non-stick frying pan with a 16cm/6 ½ inch bottom diameter generously with melted butter and place over moderately high heat. When it begins to smoke, pour in a small ladleful of batter, tilting the pan at the same time to distribute it evenly; there should only be enough to thinly coat the bottom of the pan. Cook each crêpe until lightly browned, about 30–45 seconds a side. Brush the pan with more butter as needed. Stack the cooked crêpes separated by pieces of parchment or greaseproof paper or foil, keeping them warm until all are made.

Peel and core the apples and cut them into eighths. Put them in a bowl with the 6 tbsp of melted butter and the caster (granulated) sugar. Mix to coat well. Arrange the apple pieces on a baking tray. Bake in a preheated 220°C/425°F/gas mark 7 oven for about 15 minutes, or until the edges are brown.

To assemble the crêpes, lay 12 well formed crêpes on a work surface, divide the apples between them and roll up. Arrange the filled crêpes on a serving platter and sprinkle generously with icing (confectioner's) sugar.

Note: Small apples are better than large ones in the recipe as the pieces fit more easily into the crêpes. For easier clean-up, line the baking tray with foil before cooking the apples. If preferred, the crêpes may be cooked in advance; reheat them in a moderate oven, well wrapped.

INDEX